Collins easy

Handwriting

Ages 7–9

The quick brown fox jumps over the lazy dog

Karina Law

How to use this book

- Find a quiet, comfortable place to work, away from distractions.

- Help with reading instructions to ensure that your child understands what to do.

- Encourage your child to check their handwriting as they complete each activity. Discuss with your child what they have learnt.

- Let your child return to their favourite pages once they have been completed, to talk about the activities.

- Reward your child with plenty of praise and encouragement.

- The National Curriculum states that children should be taught to understand which letters, when next to one another, are best left unjoined. These are called break letters. Some schools do teach children to join some, or all these letters. Check which handwriting style your child's school uses.

Supporting left-handed writers

- Position paper slightly to the left and tilt it clockwise.

- Help your child to rest their pencil in the 'V' between their thumb and index finger; their fingers should be between one and two centimetres away from the pencil point.

- Check with your child's school to find out how they teach letter formation; some of the strokes will be made in the opposite direction to right-handed writers.

Published by Collins
An imprint of HarperCollins*Publishers* Ltd
The News Building
1 London Bridge Street
London
SE1 9GF

Browse the complete Collins catalogue at
www.collins.co.uk

© HarperCollins*Publishers* Ltd 2011
This edition © HarperCollins*Publishers* Ltd 2015

10 9 8 7 6 5 4 3 2 1

ISBN 978-0-00-815142-3

The author asserts the moral right to be identified as the author of this work.

British Library Cataloguing in Publication Data.

A Catalogue record for this publication is available from the British Library.

Written by Karina Law
Based on content by Sue Peet
Design and layout by Linda Miles, Lodestone Publishing and Contentra Technologies Ltd
Illustrated by Graham Smith, Andy Tudor and Jenny Tulip
Cover design by Sarah Duxbury and Paul Oates
Cover illustrations © passengerz/gettyimages.co.uk and © Blue Planet Earth/gettyimages.co.uk
Project managed by Sonia Dawkins

MIX
Paper from
responsible sources
FSC™ C007454

Contents

Trace the dotted letters. Then write them out three times each.

a a a a a a a

b b b b b b b

c c c c c c

d d d d d d d d

e e e e e e e e e e

f f f

g g g

h h h

i i i

j j j

k k k

l l l

m m m

n n n

o o o

p p p

q q q

r r r

s s s

t t t

u u u

v v v

w w w

x x x

y y y

z z z

Alphabet zoo

Read each word. Then write it out twice.

ant   ant ant

bear   bear

crocodile   crocodile

donkey   donkey

elephant   elephant

frog   frog

goat   goat

hamster   hamster

iguana   iguana

jackal   jackal

kangaroo   kangaroo

lizard   lizard

meerkat   meerkat

newt   newt

ostrich   ostrich

panda   panda

quail   quail

rabbit   rabbit

snake   snake

tiger   tiger

umbrella bird   umbrella bird

vole   vole

walrus   walrus

x-ray fish   x-ray fish

yak   yak

zebra   zebra

Alphabet actions

Read each word. Then write it out three times.

acting

baking

catching

dancing

eating

flying

giving

hiding

inspecting

joking

kicking

lifting

measuring

nibbling

opening

painting

queuing

running

swimming

talking

undoing

visiting

walking

mixing

yawning

zipping

Alphabet picnic

Read each word. Then write it out twice.

apple

bread

carrot

doughnut

eggs

flapjack

grapes

honey

ice cream

jelly

kiwi fruit

lemon

muffin

nuts

orange

pizza

quiche

rice

spaghetti

tomato

upside down cake

vegetables

watermelon

box of biscuits

yoghurt

fizzy drink

Handwriting practice: the quick brown fox

The sentence below contains all the letters of the alphabet.

Write the sentence three times in your best handwriting.

The quick brown fox jumps over the lazy dog.

Make up another sentence that contains all the letters of the alphabet.

Limericks

A limerick is a funny, five-line poem with a special rhythm.

Read and write.

There was a young lady of Riga,
Who rode with a smile on a tiger;
They returned from the ride
With the lady inside,
And the smile on the face of the tiger.

Anon

Read and write.

There was an Old Man with a beard,
Who said, 'It is just as I feared!
Two Owls and a Hen,
Four Larks and a Wren,
Have all built their nests in my beard!'

Edward Lear

Sound words

Copy each sound word and say it aloud. What does it remind you of?

crunch	plop	boing
purr	cackle	snarl
clang	clatter	splat
croak	clunk	drip
glug	tick	hum

Look at the sounds words on page 14. Choose the word that best matches the picture. Write the word next to the picture.

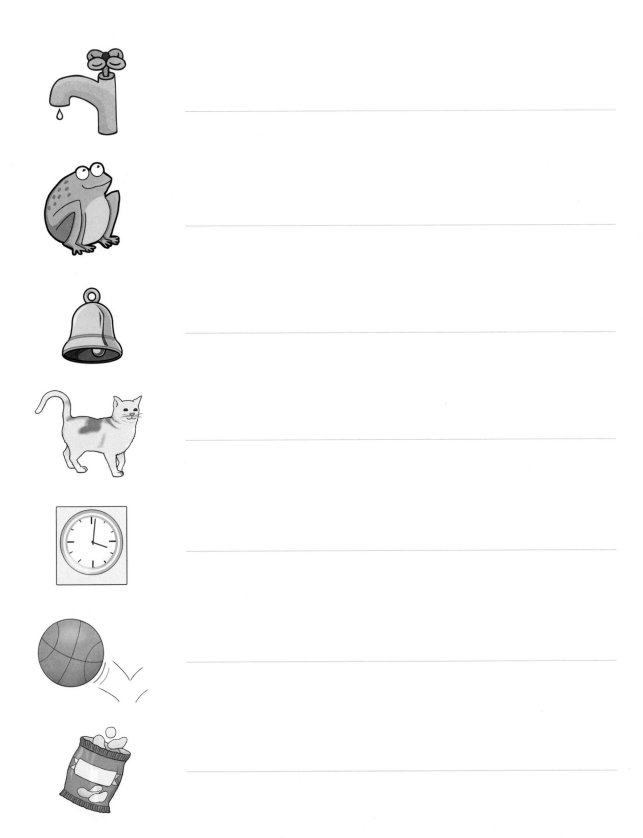

Vowel sounds: ee/ea, ie/y/igh

Read each word. Then write it out.

wheel _____   asleep _____

scream _____   beat _____

Read and write.

The queen eats peaches.

_____

_____

Read each word. Then write it out.

pie _____   tie _____

spy _____   fly _____

light _____   might _____

Read and write.

A frightened knight.

_____

_____

Vowel sounds: oa/ow, oo/ue

Read each word. Then write it out.

boat _____   float _____

yellow _____   follow _____

Copy the joke in your best handwriting.

If the sun shines while it's snowing what should you look for?
A snowbow!

_____

_____

_____

Read each word. Then write it out.

balloon _____   igloo _____

glue _____   clue _____

Copy the joke in your best handwriting.

What holds the moon up?
Moonbeams!

_____

_____

Synonyms

Synonyms are words that are similar in meaning.

Write a synonym next to each word.

rich   answer   tidy   tasty   selfish   huge
funny   handsome   quick   afraid

neat _____

delicious _____

reply _____

enormous _____

amusing _____

attractive _____

frightened _____

wealthy _____

mean _____

fast _____

Antonyms

Write an antonym next to each word.

> closed   narrow   boring   light   mean   noisy
> dirty   young   strong   beautiful

wide _____

dark _____

open _____

quiet _____

clean _____

interesting _____

old _____

weak _____

ugly _____

kind _____

Tongue twisters

Copy the tongue twister twice. Then practise reading it aloud.

Red lorry, yellow lorry. Red lorry, yellow lorry.

Copy the tongue twister twice. Then practise reading it aloud.

Hungry horses happily eating hay.

Copy the tongue twister twice. Then practise reading it aloud.

Peter Parrot pecked a painting pirate.

_____

_____

Copy the tongue twister twice. Then practise reading it aloud.

Frogs frantically flipping frisbees

_____

_____

Word endings: ing

Trace and write.

ing ~~ing~~ _____

Add ing to each word. Then write the whole word three times.

eat _____

help _____

rain _____

sing _____

sleep _____

Add ing to each word. Then write the whole word three times.

cry _____

listen _____

pull _____

kiss _____

Double the final consonant before adding ing to these words. Then write the whole word three times.

skip _____

run _____

hop _____

swim _____

hit _____

hug _____

hum _____

Greetings!

Read and write.

Happy Birthday!

_____

Happy Anniversary!

_____

Get Well Soon!

_____

Sorry You're Leaving!

_____

Happy New Year!

_____

Good Luck!

_____

Congratulations!

_____

Choose a greeting and design a card. Write the greeting neatly in the centre.

To _____

_____

From _____

Word endings: er, est

Read each word. Then write it out twice, adding er and est to the end.

small   smaller   smallest

long _____

fast _____

young _____

high _____

tall _____

strong _____

dark _____

bright _____

Read each word. Then double the final consonant before writing it out again, adding er and est.

big   bigger   biggest

wet _____

fat _____

thin _____

fit _____

hot _____

Compound words

A compound word is made up of two other words.

wheel + chair = wheelchair

Unscramble these nonsense words. Match the start of each word to the correct ending to make compound words. Write the correct words opposite.

superbird   ladyfly   wheelbow

jellyhouse   newshero

eggfish   butterchair   raincup

lightbrush   toothpaper

Read and write.

What house weighs the least?
A lighthouse!

superhero

Capital letters

Capital letters don't join to any other letter.

Trace and write. Start at the red dot.

A A A   B B   C C

D D D   E E   F F

G G G   H H   I I

J J J   K K   L L

M M M   N N   O O

P P P   Q Q   R R

S S   T T   U U

V V V   W W   X X

Y Y Y   Z Z

Team supporters

Write the team names on the scarves using capital letters.

REAL MADRID

LIVERPOOL

BARCELONA

MANCHESTER

ARSENAL

CHELSEA

Write the name of your favourite team here.

Handwriting practice: 'How doth the little crocodile'

Write this poem in your best handwriting.

How doth the little crocodile
Improve his shining tail,
And pour the waters of the Nile
On every golden scale!

How cheerfully he seems to grin
How neatly spreads his claws,
And welcomes little fishes in,
With gently smiling jaws.

Lewis Carroll